Practical Assertiveness for Professionals in Health Care:
Skills Key to Personal Effectiveness with Patients, Families and Coworkers

Wendy Leebov, Ed. D.

Leebov Golde Group

Practical Assertiveness for Professionals in Health Care:
Skills Key to Personal Effectiveness with Patients, Families and Coworkers

Requests to the Publisher for permission should be addressed to
Wendy Leebov; 625 Casa Loma Blvd., Unit 1406; Boynton Beach
FL 33435
Fax: 215-893-3524
Email: wleebov@quality-patient-experience.com;
Phone: 215-413-1969

Keywords: Patient experience, patient satisfaction, healthcare
training, service excellence, service improvement, excellent service,
service quality, patient-centered care, HCAHPS, healthcare quality,
leadership development, management development

About the Author

Wendy Leebov, Ed.D is a passionate advocate for creating healing
environments for patients, families, and the entire healthcare team
for over thirty years, Wendy Leebov has helped hospitals and
medical practices enhance the patient experience. Wendy is
currently President and CEO of the Leebov Golde Group.
Previously, she served as Vice President and change coach for the
Albert Einstein Healthcare Network in Philadelphia. A
communication fanatic, Wendy has written more than ten books for
health care, as well as toolkits, guides, instructional manuals, slide

shows, and articles.   Wendy's most recent books:

- **Wendy Leebov's Essentials for Great Personal Leadership;**
  AHA Press, 2008
- **Wendy Leebov's Essentials for Great Patient Experiences;**
  AHA Press, 2008

Wendy received her Bachelor of Arts in Sociology/Anthropology from Oberlin College and her master's and doctorate from the Harvard Graduate School of Education.

ABOUT THIS BOOK

This book is meant to help you learn the basics of assertive behavior and to use them to improve your effectiveness at work. Assertive behavior will help you cope with difficult situations on and off the job and will improve the way you deal with the people around you, making it more likely that you will get the results you want. Throughout this book you will find exercises and suggestions for role-playing to help you establish, practice and strengthen your assertive approach to work situations.

A specialist in health care staff development and customer relations wrote this book for you. The contents reflect several years of research into effective interpersonal behaviors—behaviors that can work for both you and your customers.

OTHER TITLES IN THIS SERIES:
Customer Service
Resolving Complaints
Telephone Skills
Working Together

Practical Assertiveness— Introduction

Ask yourself how you would react in each of these situations. The answer will say a great deal about how assertive you are in the face of difficult situations and how likely you are to get the results you want.

- What would you do if the only other technician in your lab always managed to find something more important to do when you were in a jam and needed help?
- What would you do if your supervisor approved time off for you but, at the last minute, seemed to want you to come in to work after all?
- How would you react if it was 10 minutes to 5 and your boss handed you a 15-page report to type before the next morning?

All of us who work in health care have run into situations very much like the ones just described. Any one of them could make us feel angry and resentful. How we deal with these situations will determine our effectiveness as workers and as co-workers, how we feel about our jobs and about ourselves, and how we feel about life in general. There is even evidence that how we deal with difficult or stressful situations in our lives also influences both our mental and physical health.

The ability to deal effectively with difficult situations is not an inborn talent. It is a learned skill. Some people who learn it early in life seem to breeze through school and social situations with complete confidence and experience only minor stress. Others have a more difficult time and become self-conscious and shy, or they always seem to feel socially awkward, not knowing the right thing to say or the best way to deal with other people and with difficult situations. Such people—and that includes most of us—must make a conscious effort later in life to learn effective ways of handling difficult situations. Fortunately it's never too late to learn behavior that can help you respond effectively. You can adopt new behaviors that improve your interpersonal relationships, enhance your self-esteem, and get you more of what you need in order to perform your job effectively and work well with others.

Sound good? It's all part of a philosophy and an approach to interpersonal interaction called assertiveness. You can choose to follow the principles of assertiveness any time you want to.

WHY BE ASSERTIVE?

Think about situations in your own life that you did or did not handle in an effective way. Why did you act the way you did? Why did some situations turn out well when others did not? Think about what the outcomes were and how you might have handled each situation differently. We all find it possible to act assertively in some situations but not in others. Most of us have particular settings in which our responses are usually assertive and other situations in which we cannot be assertive. For example, we may be able to express ourselves openly and honestly with our closest friends. But are we as open and honest with our supervisors and managers? With difficult physicians? With other people in authority? It is possible to use assertive behavior even with authority figures and others with whom we might not feel entirely comfortable.

To adopt assertiveness as our own preferred way of behaving is to adopt a means of showing respect for ourselves and respect for others. At the same time we increase the likelihood of getting what we want.

WHAT IS ASSERTIVE BEHAVIOR?

Assertive behavior, or assertiveness, is the ability to stand up for your rights and for what you want and to express your feelings, opinions and preferences openly, honestly and directly in ways that show respect for yourself and others. To do this, you must:
- Know who you are.
- Know what you want.
- Know how to get what you want.
- Believe you can get what you want.

Assertiveness is an approach to interpersonal interaction that depends on your having self-respect, a positive feeling of self-worth, and the ability to understand that you are important and you deserve to have what you want as much as the next person. The key is to go after what you want and what you believe in ways that show respect for others as well as for yourself. Many of us believe that the wants and needs of others are always much more important than our own. However, we do ourselves a disservice when we assume that, and we place others in a position of power over us that is unwarranted and that we may find uncomfortable.

One expert has spelled out a philosophy behind assertiveness with 10 basic principles:

1. When we stand up for ourselves and let ourselves be known to others, we gain greater self-respect and greater respect from others.

2. When we try to live our lives so that we never hurt anyone around us, under any circumstances, we actually wind up hurting ourselves—and others.

3. When we stand up for ourselves and express our genuine feelings in direct, honest and appropriate ways, everyone benefits in the long run.

4. When we demean or belittle others around us, we demean ourselves, and everyone loses.

5. When we share our true reactions with others and allow others to share their honest reactions with us, our personal relationships become more authentic and satisfying.

6. When we sacrifice our own integrity and deny our personal feelings, our relationships suffer or stop short of what they could be.

7. When we try to control others through guilt, hostility or intimidation, relationships are damaged.

8. When we do not let others know what we think and feel, it is just as inconsiderate as not listening to others when they express their thoughts and feelings.

9. When we repeatedly place others in a position of superiority over us, we teach people that they can take advantage of us.

10. When we act assertively and tell other people how their behavior affects us, we give them the opportunity to change, and we show them that we respect their right to know where they stand with us.

*Adapted from P. Jakubowski in "Self-Assertion Training Procedures for Women," a chapter in E. Rowlings and D. Carter, eds., *Psychotherapy for Women* Springfield, Illinois: Charles C. Thomas, 1977.

WHEN HAVE YOU BEEN ASSERTIVE?		
List four times you can recall being assertive. Evaluate how appropriate you think your response was in each situation.		
SITUATION/RESPONSE	HOW APPROPRIATE?	DID I GET RESULTS?

1.									
	1	2	3	4	5	No	Somewhat	Yes!	

2.									
	1	2	3	4	5	No	Somewhat	Yes!	

3.									
	1	2	3	4	5	No	Somewhat	Yes!	

4.									
	1	2	3	4	5	No	Somewhat	Yes!	

ARE THERE ALTERNATIVE RESPONSES?

Assertiveness is only one way to approach a situation—but usually it is the most effective way. Still, there are other options, and you may already use them, depending on the particular situation. These alternative responses include nonassertive, or passive, behavior and aggressive behavior.

Nonassertive Behavior

Nonassertive behavior usually means putting aside your own wants and needs and giving in to the needs of others. For instance, what would you do if your boss made it clear that he expected you to stay late, even if you had made other plans? Some people would submissively agree to stay, without speaking up about their other plans. This would be a nonassertive, or passive, response.

Some people would take offense at this request, showing aggressive behavior. Others might act assertively. A positive, assertive response in this situation might be: "I wasn't aware of the need to stay late tonight, and I haven't made the necessary arrangements. I would really prefer not to stay late today." If said in a straightforward manner, without anger or sarcasm, such a response could be effective and acceptable, and your boss might well find an alternative to your working late that particular time.

Still others, if they appreciate the chance to stay to finish a particular project might readily agree to stay late and feel fine about it. While saying "Yes, I can do that" might appear to be a nonassertive response, under these circumstances it is not hurtful and will not damage your self-esteem because you have chosen to accept the change in plans.

However, if you really do find staying late difficult and an unreasonable request, and you agree to do it because you are afraid to speak up about it, you are showing nonassertive, or passive, behavior.

You do have a choice about whether to engage in nonassertive behavior. Nonassertive behavior is not always undesirable. In our example, you might choose to respond non-assertively because you were late this morning and this annoyed your boss, and you don't want to risk annoying him even further right now. Or maybe you decide to be nonassertive now because you think you can use this situation later when you want to ask your boss to be flexible about your time of arrival due to an errand you want to run. You might have good reasons for going along with the request without a complaint or comment.
Nonassertive behavior is one option that you can choose to use in certain situations, and it can be an appropriate response. But know why you choose it, and make sure it's a choice.

Often non-assertiveness is not a chosen response at all, and the result is that the person who engaged in it ends up feeling resentment and anger. Many people operate in a nonassertive fashion automatically, often because they have low self-esteem and they assume that everyone else is more important than they are. They make their own wants and needs secondary to the needs of almost everyone around them. They dismiss their own feelings as unreal and unimportant and submit to others' needs in order to avoid displeasing or angering them. However, the outcome of nonassertive behavior can be very costly. If you constantly suppress your own needs and wants, you may build a growing resentment that eventually will emerge in subtle, negative behaviors that can damage your relationships with others and your professional effectiveness.

Nonassertive behavior is typical of people who rely primarily on the opinions of others for their self-esteem. This behavior permits you to always be "the good guy"—but at the expense of your own self-worth. And it can cost you the respect of others if you continually demonstrate that you consider your own needs to be unimportant.

WHEN HAVE YOU BEEN NONASSERTIVE?			
List four times you can recall being nonassertive. Evaluate how appropriate you think your response was in each situation.			
SITUATION/RESPONSE	HOW APPROPRIATE?	DID I GET RESULTS?	
1.			
	1 2 3 4 5	No Somewhat	Yes!
2.			
	1 2 3 4 5	No Somewhat	Yes!
3.			
	1 2 3 4 5	No Somewhat	Yes!
4.			
	1 2 3 4 5	No Somewhat	Yes!

Aggressive Behavior

Some people when confronted with a difficult situation, such as being asked to work late, feel threatened and resort to aggressive behavior. With aggressive behavior, like assertive behavior, you stand up for your rights, but there is one fundamental difference. With aggressive behavior you do not show respect for the feelings of others. Aggressive responses typically spring from anger and might involve sarcasm or insults designed to overpower the other person in order to get your way.

It is important to note that anger, in itself, is a normal reaction in some situations. But anger need not automatically lead to aggression or to aggressive reactions if you remain aware of your feelings and stay in control of your reactions.

For example, a person responding to a request to work late might say: "How come I always have to work late? Doesn't anyone in this department work but me? For Pete's sake, let someone else stay for a change." This type of aggressive response immediately puts the other person on the defensive and indicates an unwillingness to respect that person's position. Though it may achieve the desired short-term effect— not having to work late—it can create tension that makes maintaining long-term working relationships difficult. With aggressive behavior you may or may not get what you want, but in either case the costs can be high. You can lose the respect and the cooperation of the people around you, and you can damage your own self-respect as well.

People tend to resort to aggressive behavior when they feel threatened or when feelings of disappointment, anger or hurt become overwhelming. In fact, aggressive behavior is often characteristic of people who have low self-esteem and who do not feel in control of their own lives. They resort to bullying or lashing out at others in an attempt to gain some control.

Just as nonassertive behavior can be unproductive, aggressive behavior can be equally unproductive and even counterproductive, though for different reasons. In their attempts to succeed, aggressive responders become uncooperative and antagonistic, setting off a cycle in which nobody around them wants to cooperate with them and give them what they want. The end result is often the complete opposite of what the aggressive responder intended. Habitually responding in an aggressive manner will very likely damage your working relationships, may label you a troublemaker, and can make your job more difficult.

If you tend to respond to difficult situations in an aggressive manner, step back and take a good look at yourself, how you react, and what real benefits, if any, you derive from reacting this way. You can change by becoming more aware of your own reactions to situations and of the impact your responses have on other people.

WHEN HAVE YOU BEEN AGGRESSIVE

List four times you can recall being aggressive. Evaluate how appropriate you think your response was in each situation.								
SITUATION/RESPONSE	HOW APPROPRIATE?					DID I GET RESULTS?		
1.								
	1	2	3	4	5	No	Somewhat	Yes!
2.								
	1	2	3	4	5	No	Somewhat	Yes!
3.								
	1	2	3	4	5	No	Somewhat	Yes!
4.								
	1	2	3	4	5	No	Somewhat	Yes!

WHICH STYLE IS YOURS?

All three response types—assertive, nonassertive and aggressive— are learned early in life. That does not mean, however, that the style we learned then is the best style to get us what we want now.

People who learned aggressive behavior as children, may have learned that they could get what they wanted by manipulating and intimidating others. They then become aggressive adults who still use manipulation and intimidation to obtain what they want. Nonassertive responders may have learned that their feelings, needs and wants did not matter when compared to those of siblings, parents or classmates. Non-assertive types found out early that, "not making waves," was the best method to keep everyone around them content. As adults they may still take a back seat to others, and though they appear to be devoted friends, workers and family members, they may feel disappointed that they have sacrificed their needs for the needs of others. The point is that what may have been appropriate behavior early in our lives may no longer be helping us to achieve our goals as adults.

By comparison, there are those whose early environment fostered assertiveness, openness and honesty. These people tend to grow up confident and able to take on responsibility effectively. They seem to be in control of their own lives. They communicate honestly, directly and respectfully.

Regardless of the style of response you grew up with, you can learn to be assertive. You can learn to look at yourself and situations in a different way and identify the behaviors that get in the way of your interpersonal effectiveness. Most important, you can use these new behaviors both in your personal life and in your health care work.

Before you decide that you are going to be more assertive, you have to have a pretty good idea where you are going with this change, and where it is you're coming from. By now you probably have some idea about whether your characteristic response style is nonassertive, aggressive or assertive. To give yourself a clearer idea, go through the examples of different behaviors described on the next page. Each statement is identified as assertive, nonassertive or aggressive. As you read the statements, you will probably see patterns emerging, and you may even see yourself or some of your co-workers in the examples. If you look over these examples carefully, you will see that aggressive, nonassertive and assertive responses are quite different, and each has its own characteristics.

RECOGNIZING YOUR RESPONSE STYLE

1. You are working at your desk, concentrating on entering notes on a member's medical chart. Nearby, two of your co-workers are talking and laughing in loud voices that you find distracting. Your response is:

a. Looking up and saying, in an angry voice, "Can't you keep it down? Don't you see I'm trying to work?"—Aggressive
b. Doing nothing, but gritting your teeth, wishing they'd go away so you could finish your work.—Nonassertive
c. Going over to them and saying, "I know you're really involved in what you're talking about, and you probably don't realize how loud you're talking, but I'd really appreciate it if you would keep your

voices down so I can concentrate on what I'm doing."—Assertive

2. A patient's family member calls almost every 30 minutes to check on the patient's condition. You can't give her any more information than you already gave during the first phone call of the day, and, frankly, you're getting a little annoyed. The next time the person calls, your response is:

a. Assuring her that there has been no change and that if a change does occur, you will call and   let her know.—Assertive
b. Raising your voice and telling her angrily that the phone calls are really getting annoying and that if there is any change, somebody will let her know.—Aggressive
c. Quietly taking the call and repeating what you've told the caller on all the previous calls and then hanging up and mumbling to yourself and others how annoying this person is.—Nonassertive

3. Your boss hands you a 15-page paper to type at 4:45 and expects you to have it on her desk by 10:00 the following morning. She says she needs it for a presentation at a conference the following day. Your response is:

a. Gritting your teeth and typing the paper, knowing full well you'll probably have to work until 7:00 to get it even halfway done and resenting being placed in this situation.—Nonassertive
b. Saying sarcastically, "You've gotta be kidding! What am I, a magician? You knew you had this deadline a month ago. Why do I have to suffer because you leave everything until the last minute?"—Aggressive
c. Saying, "I'll give it my best shot, but I want you to know that I have to leave at 5:00, and I don't honestly feel you're being fair with me to give me such short notice."—Assertive

4. You're in a staff meeting, and your boss suggests a plan to reorganize the department's work. He thinks the plan is terrific, and it might be— if the staff were made up of programmed robots. You think it will never work as presented, and you see some ways that would make it more realistic. Your response is:

a. Turning to the co-worker sitting next to you and saying in a whisper loud enough for everyone to hear, "This is ridiculous. He's gotta be crazy!"—Aggressive

b. Speaking up and addressing the issue directly, saying that you really don't think this plan will work and presenting your modifications respectfully, without making your boss look foolish.—Assertive

c. Listening quietly, inwardly dreading having this plan go into effect and thinking that your boss must be some kind of jerk to have even thought the plan up.—Nonassertive

5. The patient in Room 518 is so demanding that you're in her room every 10 minutes to respond to the call button. It's hard to concentrate on all the other work you have to do, especially when her requests seem frivolous to you. You would like her to be more considerate of your time and less dependent on you to do things for her. Your response is:

a. Saying nothing, because you know how sick the patient is and you don't want to upset her.—Nonassertive

b. Telling her, "Look, I can't be running in here all the time. Other people need my attention, too. I think you're being very selfish by calling me every 10 minutes with these silly requests."—Aggressive

c. Telling her firmly but nicely that you are very busy with other patients as well as with her; that you are asking her to respect other people's time; and that you don't mind attending to her but that she should first consider whether the call is really necessary or can wait until you stop in next.—Assertive

6. A patient has appeared at your desk, complaining loudly about his bill. He thinks your medical practice has overcharged him, and he is demanding a revised bill. Your response is:

a. Apologizing profusely while the customer rants and raves and taking the blame on yourself or sitting there quietly, saying nothing but seething inside.—Nonassertive

b. Yelling back, becoming defensive, and arguing that if the customer had read the bill carefully, he'd understand what all the charges mean or blaming the problem on a co-worker's inefficiency and calling it another fine example of bungling by someone else.— Aggressive

c. Listening carefully to the customer's complaint to understand exactly what is being said and then, in a supportive, empathetic way, repeating the complaint back to him so that you both know you understand the problem and can address the issue point by point.— Assertive

To summarize the three response options:

- Aggressive responses are often hurtful, sarcastic and manipulative, and they may make others feel guilty or look foolish. The responses are antagonistic. They may make people do what you want them to do this time, but in the long term, aggressive responses will make people feel wary of you, resent you, and not want to cooperate with you. In short, they may backfire and damage your effectiveness.

- Nonassertive responses generally hurt nobody but you. If your style is nonassertive you may be in for a great deal of stress. People who do not speak up and who tend to keep everything inside can develop stress-related illnesses, from headaches to heart problems. Nonassertive responses can serve to make others feel guilty, but that doesn't do anything positive for them or for you. Or people may like having you around because they are able to manipulate you, and they often won't resist the temptation to take advantage of you. Nonassertive behavior is often a nonproductive approach that can leave you feeling cheated because you rarely get what you want.

- Assertive responses are honest, straightforward and often helpful—to others and to yourself. To respond assertively means that you stand up for your rights, and that you have the confidence and self-assurance to expect that others will respect you and your needs.

The consequences of each of these behaviors are illustrated in the Summary of Options and Outcomes.

SUMMARY OF OPTIONS AND OUTCOMES

NONASSERTIVE:
- Characteristics: You do not express your honest wants, ideas and feelings, or you express them in self-demeaning ways.
- You feel: anxious, disappointed with yourself, often angry and resentful after the fact.
- Others feel about you: They may like you because they can

manipulate you, but they don't respect you.

- Outcome: You don't get what you want; anger builds.
- Payoff: You've avoided unpleasant conflict tension and confrontation.

AGGRESSIVE:

- Characteristics: You express your wants, ideas and feelings in a confrontational way, at the expense of others.
- You feel: self-righteous, superior but sometimes embarrassed later.
- Others feel about you: humiliation, hurt or anger.
- Outcome: You may often get what you want but always at the expense of others, which makes others unwilling to cooperate with you.
- Payoff: You vent your anger and temporarily feel superior. However, in the long run you lose the respect and cooperation of others.

ASSERTIVE:

- Characteristics: You express wants, ideas and feelings in direct and appropriate ways.
- You feel: confident, good about yourself at the time and later.
- Others feel about you: usually respect.
- Outcome: You often get what you want.
- Payoff: You feel good, respected by others, with improved confidence and increased quality in your relationships.

Becoming Assertive

You Have a Choice!

You can choose to be assertive, nonassertive or aggressive. The choice is yours. You are not a victim of circumstances or of other people's behavior toward you. You are the one who chooses how to respond to particular situations and to the behavior of others. You may think: "Sure, I'd like to be different. But this is me, this is how I am, and this is the way I'll always be." That doesn't have to be the case. You probably know people you can identify as assertive, and perhaps you have felt you would like to be a little more like them. Many people have already learned to change their nonproductive habits through assertiveness training and through practice.

You can, too!

DOES CHANGE MEAN RISKS?

Change is always risky, and changing from passive or aggressive behavior to assertive behavior will have its risks. Here are a few points to consider:

- You won't always choose the perfect assertive response. Everyone makes mistakes. It takes practice to be able to identify responses that will work for you, and the situations and people with whom they will work. Like anything else, developing an assertive style takes practice. If you really make an effort to do things differently, assertiveness will become second nature.

- Even if you are assertive, you may not always get what you want. Assertiveness does not guarantee 100 percent success in obtaining what you want. But being assertive will improve your chances of succeeding. And there's an added bonus: As you get better at assertiveness, you'll find that you feel better about yourself. With increased self-respect, you will find that you gain greater respect from others.

Some people won't like your new behavior. Face it, some people didn't like you or treat you very well before you practiced assertiveness. Even our best friends feel uneasy when we change the way we do things or exhibit new behaviors. It's only natural; people get used to us the way they have always known us. If you used to be nonassertive or passive, some people might have liked you because they could dominate you or take advantage of you. If you were aggressive, people might have liked you because you said and did things that they never dared to say or do. But people usually don't lose true friends or the respect of competent co-workers and supervisors by changing for the better. And assertiveness is better. Though some friends and co-workers may be thrown off balance when you change, in time most will come to respect you even more.

If and When You Are Assertive, What Risks Do You Face?

Ask yourself what you are afraid of if and when you are assertive. On the list below, check those concerns you have. Then, next to each, jot down a thought you can have (something you can say to yourself) to reduce your concern.

MY CONCERN: A THOUGHT TO COUNTERACT IT?
- *I'm afraid I won't do a good job of being assertive.*

- *I'm afraid I'll be assertive, but I won't get what I want anyway.*

- *I'm afraid some people won't like my behavior.*

- *I'm afraid some people will lose respect for me.*

- *I'm afraid the other person will argue with me and I won't know how to handle it.*

Change takes practice. If you try to be assertive once or twice and feel uneasy or find that you do not get the reaction you want, just keep practicing. Eventually, you will catch on and become aware that your relationship with the world around you—and with yourself—is changing for the better! After all, the key to assertiveness is respect for yourself and for others.

DO YOU THINK ASSERTIVELY?	
Instructions: Read each statement and circle the number from one to five that best describes you. A one means that you never feel this way and a five means that you always feel this way.	
I believe my needs are as important as the needs of others and that I have a right to act in my own best interest.	1 2 3 4 5
I feel at ease and confident speaking before a group.	1 2 3 4 5
When people around me act in ways that bother, upset or anger me, I tell	1 2 3 4 5

them so without feeling self-conscious or guilty.	
I readily admit when I've made a mistake and am not ashamed.	1 2 3 4 5
I can and do voice my opinions to my supervisor and others in authority.	1 2 3 4 5
In meetings or social situations, when I don't agree with what others are saying, I can stand my ground without feeling anxious or self-conscious.	1 2 3 4 5
I feel confident that I can learn to do new things.	1 2 3 4 5
I can express my anger without making others feel guilty about making me angry.	1 2 3 4 5
I am at ease meeting new people socially.	1 2 3 4 5
I can talk easily about my feelings,	1 2 3 4 5

including uncomfortable ones like anger, frustration and disappointment.	
When someone asks me to do something I really don't want to do, I can say no to them without feeling guilty.	1 2 3 4 5
When others express beliefs that are different from my own, I can respect them, and I don't try to make the other person feel they are wrong, stupid or irrational for holding those beliefs.	1 2 3 4 5
I expect others to be competent and trustworthy, and I have no difficulty delegating responsibility to them.	1 2 3 4 5
I can ask others to do things without feeling anxious or guilty.	1 2 3 4 5
I feel confident	1 2 3 4 5

and in control speaking up in meetings and groups.	
TOTAL:	

Your Score: Add up all the numbers you've circled. The highest possible score is 75. If you scored 60 or better, your assertive philosophy is already quite strong. Reading this booklet will help to reinforce that tendency.

If you scored 45 to 59, you are fairly assertive and use an assertive approach in many but not all situations. You can benefit from learning more about assertiveness and from practice.

If you scored 30 to 44, you have a good working knowledge of assertive behavior but are probably more often nonassertive or aggressive in your responses to interpersonal situations. This booklet can help strengthen your assertive approach and your perceptions of yourself in relation to others.

With a score of 15 to 29, you have some difficulty being assertive and may have problems with self-esteem. You may need a different way of looking at yourself and your relationships with others. Keep reading. This booklet may help you see things in ways you haven't considered!

WHAT ARE YOUR ASSERTIVE RIGHTS?

Before you can stand up for your assertive rights, you need to know what they are. Every individual has certain rights that we will refer to as your 10 basic assertive rights. As you read them, you will become aware that others around you exercise these rights. Now you are going to focus on exercising them yourself.

Your 10 Basic Assertive Rights:

1. You have the right to act in ways that promote your own dignity and self-respect. You can choose the values you will live by, and you can choose your lifestyle—as long as you don't violate the rights of others. You have the right to be yourself and to act in ways that promote your self-respect. When you accept this right and choose to act on it, you feel better about yourself and enjoy your relationships more. And you are able to deal effectively with those who violate your rights, and to respond in ways that acknowledge their rights as well.

2. You have the right to be treated with respect by everyone with whom you interact. If someone abuses this right, you have the right to insist on respect. Treating each other with respect promotes equality in relationships and gives each person an opportunity to feel good and to grow.

3. You have the right to experience and express your thoughts and emotions. Emotions give depth and richness to our lives. They are neither good nor bad. You may be exercising a kind of self-talk that puts down your own feelings—"I shouldn't be angry at her" or "I shouldn't feel hurt." In fact, emotions can be directly related to real situations: You may feel angry because your coworker has taken a few days off and left you with more than your share of the work. Or emotions can come from within us, with little or no relationship to outside events. When this happens, they can momentarily make us feel confused or anxious for no apparent reason. Censoring your emotions and trying to deny them can lead to nonassertive behavior, low self-esteem, and an inability to act in your own best interest. Denying your emotions can also lead you to act aggressively and to respond in ways that are not appropriate to the specific situation. Be aware of your emotions and try to understand why you feel them.

Also, try to learn when it may be a good idea to put off important decisions and reactions until you feel more in control.

4. You have the right to slow down and make conscious, not impulsive, decisions. Tune in to your feelings before you act. It may take just a moment or it may take longer, but be sure you understand why you are taking an action or responding in a certain way. And be sure that the decision you make will be in your best interest, as well as in the best interest of the other people involved. You are not taking care of yourself responsibly if you always react with spur-of-the-moment decisions. Obviously, there will be times when you must react instantly, but if you take time to think through how you want to handle a situation, you will get better results. Taking time to choose your approach will become easier with practice. As you become more adept at tuning in to your emotions and needs, you will be able to weigh the alternatives and still respond quickly.

5. You have the right to ask for what you want. If you respect the rights of others—and that means you are not going to ask for something that violates the rights of others—you will at least get a fair hearing. A lot of people—and you may be one of them—feel guilty when they ask for what they want. But you are responsible for yourself, and other people are responsible for themselves. If others do or do not want to give you what you want, then let them speak responsibly for themselves. "But what if I ask and I'm rejected?" you might wonder. That's a legitimate fear. You can't always expect to get what you ask for; that's a risk that we take. But you'll rarely get what you want if you don't ask for it.

6. You have the right to say no. Whether you exercise it or not, you always have—and always have had—the right to say no. Saying no doesn't make you a bad person. Someone else's right to ask you for something is no greater or more important than your right to refuse them. People may not like it when you refuse their requests, but that doesn't mean they don't like you personally. You may find some negative reaction when you first start to exercise this right, but if you also respect other people's rights when saying no, people will eventually come to understand that you are standing up for yourself, and they will respect you for it.

7.   You have the right to change your mind. You may make a decision quickly or under pressure and then, after you've had time to give it additional thought, decide that it is not the best thing to do. That's OK. Just about everyone changes their mind sometimes. It doesn't mean that you're wishy-washy or that you don't know your own mind. It may turn out that your revised decision is better accepted by others than the first. Many legal contracts now allow a grace period for the involved parties to rethink a decision that is legally binding. The right to change your mind is generally respected. It's important that you exercise your right to change your mind when you feel that you initially made a mistake.

8.   You have the right to be less than perfect. Everyone wants to do their best at whatever they undertake, but few of us can be perfect at everything we do—and certainly not 100 percent of the time. We all have days when our energy or attention isn't exactly what we want it to be. You have a right to have bad days, or downtime, to be imperfect, and to do less well in some things than you do in others. This is important because very often, trying to be the best all the time means doing for others at a cost to yourself.

9.   You have the right to make mistakes. It isn't the end of the world if you make a mistake or are wrong about something. Mistakes are inevitable, and everyone makes them. Feeling bad about making mistakes really isn't going to help you stop making them. Instead, it may make you so self-conscious that you mess up even more. If you are going to be more assertive, you will have to accept the fact that you will make some mistakes, learn how to acknowledge them when you do, and see them as opportunities to learn and grow.

10. You have the right to feel good about yourself. Feeling good about yourself is really what being assertive is all about. Many people feel guilty or shy about saying positive things about themselves or their successes. Saying good things about yourself isn't always bragging. Talking openly and honestly about your accomplishments is fine, and it helps others to know you better.

Similarly, there is nothing to be gained from emphasizing your weaknesses. You have the same right as others to feel good about yourself, to be proud of your achievements, and to express your good feelings to *others*.

(Adapted from The Assertive Option: Your Rights and Responsibilities, by Patricia Jakubowski and Arthur J. Lange (Champaign, Illinois: Research Press Company, 1978, pp. 79-90).)

To exercise these rights and to protect them, you must learn to stand up for yourself and express your feelings, opinions and preferences. That is not as easy as it sounds, but with practice it will become easier and easier.

Here are some other rights you may want to consider adopting as your own:
- You have the right to be treated and respected as an individual, with unique values, skills and needs.
- You have the right to have your own feelings and opinions.
- You have the right to say "I don't know" when you don't know.
- You have the right to feel angry.
- You have the right to make decisions regarding your own life.
- You have the right to recognize that your needs are as important as the needs of others.

HOW DO YOU CHANGE YOUR BEHAVIOR?

To change your behavior and establish your assertive rights, you can start by thinking of yourself as your own best friend. Surely, you would want to please your best friend and do what is best for him or her. It's time to start thinking of yourself that way, as someone worthy of your attention and support. There are a number of approaches you can take to change your behavior. You can begin by showing yourself respect, by using "I" statements and other assertive messages, by using follow-up techniques, by practicing assertiveness, by learning how to accept criticism as well as compliments, and by learning how to handle conflict situations.

Showing Yourself Respect

It is possible to convince others that you are worthy of respect, but when you do not believe it yourself, this impression soon fades. That is why, before you even begin to change your behavior toward others, you must change your behavior toward yourself. You must learn to truly respect and value yourself, to treat yourself with kindness, intelligence and consideration. You show yourself respect by:

- Putting limits on what you are willing to do for others.
- Realistically evaluating situations—distinguishing between imagined fear and real danger—and dealing effectively with situations without being overwhelmed.
- Understanding the limits of what you can accomplish and doing the best you can do without having unrealistic expectations of yourself.
- Keeping control of your anger so that you don't hurt others and wind up feeling disappointed with yourself.
- Rewarding yourself for small gains in assertive skills and in other areas of your life that you are trying to improve.
- Not becoming depressed or upset if someone treats you unfairly.
- Forgiving yourself for not always living up to your promises to yourself.
- Not responding to difficult times by reverting back to nonassertive or aggressive behavior.

Work through the next exercise to see how you rate yourself and your good qualities. Another good exercise is to rewrite your resume—not because you are looking for a new job, but because it requires you to evaluate your positive qualities.

Many people think they should be humble when preparing a resume, that bragging is inappropriate. Modesty has its place, but when you are competing against others, you have to be very assertive and direct about your good qualities and what you can contribute to a new organization. In this case, you are rewriting your resume in order to reassess your own self-worth.

Pull out your last resume and think seriously about how you can make yourself sound on paper like the absolute best at what you do. See what qualifications and skills you could add that would make you the most desirable candidate for a job. Have you really listed all of your qualifications and accomplishments? Don't be modest. The more you concentrate on your good qualities and real accomplishments, the more you will respect yourself.

Review Your Good Qualities

Instructions: Write the words "I am" and beneath that list the numbers 1 through 10. Concentrate deeply on the words "I am," and when you are ready, write in the 10 spaces 10 positive qualities that you are absolutely sure make you worthy of self-respect and the respect of those around you. For example, start with 'I am" and list your positive qualities:

1. Competent	6. Responsible
2. Smart	7. Funny
3. Upbeat	8. Optimistic
4. Hard-working	9. Honest
5. Loyal	10. Caring

_____

_____

_____

_____

_____

_____

You may borrow from this list, but it would be better to use your own words to describe the qualities that contribute to making you the wonderful person that you are and that your friends respect. You may find it a little difficult at first to think up 10 items, and you may feel self-conscious about doing this. But if you do this at least once every week, you will find it easier to fill in the blanks. Every time you perform this exercise, you will strengthen your feelings of self-worth and self-respect.

Even if you are shy about talking about yourself, do it anyway! We have all been astonished at times at how some people can brag about themselves. Well, you can do it, too, without being obnoxious about it. It helps to let people know you have done something special, that you are someone special.

Of course, not everyone is always going to like you. Nobody has that kind of record. But you will not know how much people will like you if you do not make it a point to know yourself and your own good qualities. Give them a chance to get to know the whole you.

BUILD YOUR SKILLS: LEARN TO USE "I" STATEMENTS

Using "I" Statements and Other Assertive Messages

The preceding section discussed your relationship with yourself and learning to respect yourself. This section discusses enhancing your relationship with others once you are confident enough in your own self-worth to practice assertiveness in real-life situations. You can begin by learning how to use "I" statements.

Most of the time when we have something to say about another person's behavior, we say it by using "you" messages. "You" messages include statements like "You didn't follow through" or "You're acting like a child" or "You're making me nervous." Sometimes these messages take the form of threats—"If you don't stop..., I'll..." The results of these messages, though they may or may not change behavior momentarily, are that the other person feels uncomfortable or defensive and actually becomes resistant to change.

A more effective approach, one grounded in assertiveness, is the "I" message. This message allows you to describe the behavior of the other person and express the negative effect this behavior has on you. Then it leaves it up to the other person to modify the behavior or not, depending on whether they want to have the effect you described. Using an "I" message helps you to cut to the core of the issue and handle differences without bullying or blaming others or immediately defending yourself.

There are seven basic forms of "I" messages.

"I Want" Statements

Purpose: To clarify what you want of yourself and of others. It tells people what you want to do or what you want them to do. If their needs conflict with yours, you can negotiate to reach a compromise.

Examples:
- I want to know what I did to make you angry so that we can discuss it.
- I'd like you to be on time when we have an appointment.

- I'd like you to help me prepare the bibliography for Dr. Melnick's research paper.
- I'd really appreciate it if you would handle the medications this evening so I can catch up on paperwork.

Result: Others know exactly what you want and how to fulfill your requests.

Practice "I Want" Statements

Think of someone you're having problems with at work. List below three "I want" statements that you would like to say to this person.

1._____

_____

2._____

_____

3._____

_____

"I Feel" Statements

Purpose: To let you express your feelings without making others feel inferior or inadequate. Being able to express your feelings openly helps others to understand you and the consequences of their actions, and this in turn helps them.

Examples:

- I feel grateful to you for helping me on the floor tonight.
- I feel overwhelmed when you leave me in the lab alone at the busiest time of the day.
- I feel disappointed that we won't be working second shift together after this week.
- I feel much more in control when you give me some idea what the workload will be like for the rest of the week.

Results: Others know how you feel and are much more likely to respect your feelings.

Practice "I Feel" Statements

Think of someone at work whom you appreciate. Write below an "I feel" statement that expresses your positive feelings about this person.

_____

_____

_____

_____

_____

(Tell them! They'll love it!)

"Mixed Feelings" Statements

Purpose: To clear up confusion. Often, we feel both positively and negatively about a situation. There is a tendency to act on only half of these feelings—acting as though we are in agreement, when we really have strong doubts. Usually, other people sense the conflict but do not know what it's about. So, they also feel confused. The mixed feelings statement allows you to present both sides of what you are feeling, so that people can understand your feelings and your actions more clearly.

Examples:
- I'm happy with my salary increase, and I'm grateful that you appreciate my work. But it bothers me that my salary is still below that of others in the same position.
- I'm flattered that you ask me to do projects like this research, but I'm concerned that it falls into a higher job description than I've been working at thus far, and I would like my job upgraded.

Results: You made it clear that you are not completely comfortable with a situation that looks from one point of view quite positive but from the other has shortcomings. It is a far superior approach to saying nothing or expressing only one side.

One further comment: You may choose to share one feeling and get feedback on it before introducing the other side of it. That way you can test out your feelings and possibly strengthen one or the other side. Just be sure to make both your feelings known.

Practice "Mixed Feelings" Statements

Think of an issue that comes up at work about which you have mixed feelings. On the lines below, practice finding the words to express these mixed feelings.

_____

_____

_____

_____

_____

_____

_____

_____

_____

_____

Flat-Out "No" Statements

Purpose: To state clearly and emphatically that the answer is no. This is often not an easy thing to do.
Examples:

- No.

- As I said, the answer is no!

- Please understand; this is simply out of the question.

Results: Whatever the request was, you have stated clearly and emphatically that you will not comply with it. But before you say no, be absolutely sure that is what you mean. If you are not sure, take more time to think it over. If you need more information, get it. The other person may try to engage you in an argument. Actually, you do not owe the person any explanation. If you choose to give a reason, fine. But if the other person rejects your reason or disagrees, that does not mean you have to back down. In fact, you may not even know why you are saying no. That's OK, too. That's your right. You have the right to say no and to make it stick.

Practice Flat-Out "No" Statements

When a griping co-worker asks you to go to lunch, do you say yes when you'd rather say no? When your boss asks you to stay late when you already have other plans, do you say yes when you really want to say no? Most people say yes at times when they would really like to say no. See if you can list three situations you find yourself in where you do what you don't want to do or commit to something you don't want to commit to.

1._____

_____

2._____

_____

3._____

_____

Empathetic Assertion Statements

Purpose: To express sensitivity and understanding. Empathetic statements are especially important in health care settings, where patients frequently need to know that you understand and that they are not alone in their feelings. Empathetic statements also help coworkers and others know that they are not alone and that you care about them.

Examples:

- Doctor, I know it's hard for you to predict exactly when you'll be making rounds today, but I would like to go with you so I can discuss my concerns about Mr. Kramer's recovery.
- I can see that you're frustrated because your dinner was cold. Let me call Dietary Services for you and have another one sent up immediately.
- You seem upset that Mrs. Gordon spoke to you that way, and I can't blame you. It's just that her son had a relapse.

Results: People know that you understand how they are feeling, and this lessens their tendency to be defensive. They sense that you are accepting, not judgmental, about their feelings. An empathetic statement can do a lot to dissolve hostile feelings. But keep your empathetic statement short—it's enough just to let someone know you understand their feelings. If you stretch the statement out too far, you will both lose sight of what you're really talking about. And be specific about what it is you understand. For example, "I realize that you feel hurt by my criticism." This acknowledges that you not only know how the person feels, but that you also understand why the person feels as he or she does.

Practice Empathetic Assertions

Think about the customers you have served in the last two or three days. Identify three times a customer expressed emotion to you, through nonverbal gestures, tone of voice or choice of words. Below, describe the situations. Then, for each one, write down what you consider to be a tactful, empathetic assertion you might make in a similar situation in the future.

Example:

Situation—Secretary calls storeroom and, in an annoyed tone, asks, "Where is that box of supplies I ordered?"
Empathetic Assertion by storeroom clerk—"I realize it's frustrating to wait for delivery of something you need. I promise you that you'll have it this afternoon."

SITUATION 1:

_____

_____

Empathetic Assertion:

_____

_____

SITUATION 2:

_____

_____

Empathetic Assertion:

_____

_____

SITUATION 3:

_____

_____

Empathetic Assertion:

_____

_____

Confrontational Assertion Statements

Purpose: To clarify what was said before and what you want from the person now or in the future. If you have made it clear to someone what you want him or her to do, and he or she agrees to do it and then fails to, you can reiterate your position with a confrontational assertion.

Examples:

- You asked for our suggestions about how to reorganize the lab for greater efficiency, but you haven't acted on what we've said. I would like to discuss lab reorganization at our next meeting.
- You said that if I assumed the billing responsibilities I would get a raise. It's been three months, and I haven't gotten my raise. I would like to be assured that it will start with the next pay period.
- I thought we agreed we would switch lunch hours. I would appreciate it if you would stick to that.

Result: You have stated that you are bothered by the other person's behavior, and you have been specific about what that behavior is. When possible, try to find out what happened—why the person did not take the actions promised. Then, because you are not attacking the other person for his or her behavior, you are not likely to provoke defensiveness. Speak directly but without anger or hostility.

Practice Confrontational Assertion Statements

Think of a commitment or promise a co-worker made to you that he or she didn't keep. Plan the language you could use to confront them about this and write it down below.
The facts:

_____
_____
_____
_____
_____

My feelings about it:

_____
_____
_____
_____
_____

What I want:

_____
_____
_____
_____
_____

"I" Message Statements

Purpose: To address a specific, concrete behavior and the effect it had on you. The "I" message is especially effective when you want to express difficult negative feelings and give other people feedback about how their actions have affected you. If handled properly, it will probably help the other person reconsider, with a minimum of embarrassment or defensiveness, a behavior that is a problem for you. Statements that start with the following words provide the basic format: "When you...I feel..." or "Because...I want..."

Examples:

- Dr. Allen, when you yell at me, I feel angry because I find it humiliating and disrespectful. I'm very willing to listen to you, but I want you to stop yelling at me.
- When you give me the material for these reports at the last minute, I feel frustrated because I have less time to do them properly. I would appreciate it if you would coordinate the material earlier so that I can have enough time to do the reports correctly.

Results: The other person, who really may not be aware of his or her actions or their impact on others, becomes aware of specific behaviors that interfere with smooth operations and effective working relationships. You have pointed out specific ways the person can change his or her behavior, at least with regard to you. You also have left it up to the other person to decide whether to change.

Remember, you may not always get what you want, but you are much more likely to get what you want by saying what you want than by failing to make your needs known. Skill and ease in using these assertive messages will not come all at once. Using assertive messages effectively takes thought and practice. But eventually the technique will become easier to use and more habitual. Here are some tips to remember when using these assertive messages:

- Maintain direct eye contact.
- Speak clearly.
- Don't plead.
- Use gestures and facial expressions for emphasis.
- Keep your posture straight.
- Be sure your timing is appropriate.
- Don't whine or apologize.
- Be proud of yourself.

Practice "I" Message Statements

List three co-workers. Next to each, write an "I" message statement that you could beneficially say to this person to raise a concern or express an appreciation

Person 1: _____
When you _____
I feel _____
Because _____
PERSON 2: _____
When you _____
I feel _____
Because _____
PERSON 3: _____
When you _____
I feel _____
Because _____

USING FOLLOW-UP TECHNIQUES

Every plan has its pitfalls, and the basic assertive messages are no different. You will not always get what you ask for, and your assertive approaches will not always work. But you need not worry as long as you give it your best shot.

- What would you do if the only other technician in your lab always managed to find something more important to do when you were in a jam and needed help?
- What would you do if your supervisor approved time off for you but, at the last minute, seemed to want you to come in to work after all?
- How would you react if it was 10 minutes to 5 and your boss handed you a 15-page report to type before the next morning?

All of us who work in health care have run into situations very much like the ones just described. You do not need to back down just because someone was unresponsive to your assertive approach.

There are a few powerful follow-up techniques you can use:

The Broken Record:

Persistence is the key to the broken record technique—persistence and repetition, delivered in a calm, nonthreatening way. All you do is repeat your "I" message as many times as necessary to get your point across. For example:

You: I need to finish this report.
Co-worker: You can't do that now. We have to get ready for the meeting.
You: I need to finish this report. I'll still have time to get the Work together for the meeting when I'm finished with the report.
Co-worker: But I'd like to review the material for the meeting and make sure we're really prepared.
You: I know you're a bit nervous, but we've gone over the material several times, and you are in great shape to score the points you want to make. I need to finish this report before we go to the meeting.

The broken record is a simple technique that allows you to make perfectly clear what it is you want without wavering or backing down.

Fogging:

Fogging is a technique that can be used with someone who persistently criticizes, insults or complains, even after you have realized that they do not intend to do anything to resolve what they are complaining about. With fogging, you vaguely (foggily) agree with the other
Person's statements as much as possible until they give up, give in, or go away. Here is an example:

Co-worker:	Things are terrible around here.
You:	Perhaps so.
Co-worker:	Nobody cares about anything anymore.
You:	Perhaps not.
Co-worker:	My supervisor picks on me constantly.
You:	That may be.
Co-worker:	This place is a mess and nobody does anything about it.
You:	Sometimes it is messy here.

This technique is good for diffusing hostility and works best after everything else has been tried but has failed.

Unhooking:

Unhooking is an exercise in standing your ground without getting caught up in another person's reasons for why you should do what they are asking you to do. Like the broken record technique, it involves repetition and calm insistence, but the circumstances are apt to be more complicated. For example, if you are asked to do something that violates organization policy, is not part of your job, or is beyond your skill level, unhooking will help the other person to digest that your refusal is not negotiable:

Doctor:	I need you to give this medication IV every four hours.
Nurse:	Not without the attending physician's approval.
Doctor:	Don't argue with me. It's done on all the other floors, and I expect you to do it here.
Nurse:	It may be done on other floors. On this floor, I must have the attending physician's approval. She can be reached on her beeper. If she can't be reached, perhaps you should continue this discussion with my nurse manager.

PRACTICING ASSERTIVENESS

You need to practice assertiveness in real life at some point, but you can begin by "replaying" to yourself situations that have already taken place. Think of a situation that made you feel awkward or uncomfortable or one that you left without getting what you wanted. It may have been an interaction with a co-worker, a supervisor, a patient or a physician. Focus on that incident and try to remember all the details of the interaction. Write down all the steps that took place and how you felt at each step. And write down how you felt at the end of the interaction. Did you feel disappointed? Even cheated? Did you feel you wanted to start the interaction all over again and do it differently? This is your chance! Take the interaction from the top, stating exactly what you wanted the outcome to be. Then review the interaction with you in control, and replay the conversation as you wish it had evolved. Even if you could not get exactly what you wanted, would you end the interaction feeling absolutely sure you had handled it in the best possible way?

Do you have the confidence to interact assertively this way in real life? If not, keep practicing.

Practice this technique with several past incidents until you are ready to try assertiveness in new situations. Calmly and straightforwardly, tell others what you want and act as though you expect to get it.

DETERMINING OBSTACLES TO ASSERTIVENESS
Instructions: Ask a co-worker to ask you the following questions to examine more closely your specific obstacles to adopting assertiveness as a way of life. These questions will also help you identify concrete areas that you can work on to build up your assertive philosophy.
1. In what specific situations do you feel comfortable being assertive?
2. In what situations do you find it especially difficult to be assertive?

3.	What emotions do you associate with these situations? Anger? Fear? Guilt? Sadness?
4.	What are the causes of your nonassertive behavior?
5.	Describe a situation in which you would like to be more assertive. Exactly what could you do in this situation to help yourself feel or act more assertive?
6.	Think of a situation in which you fall short of behaving assertively, and write down assertive statements that would help you to handle that situation better. Practice using the statements by role-playing the situation with your co-worker.

ACCEPTING CRITICISM

Just as you are about to be assertive with others, others are going to be assertive with you. Being on the receiving end of other people's requests sometimes makes people uneasy. One situation that most people have difficulty dealing with is accepting criticism.

You can accept criticism without cringing, without feeling that you have been put down or hurt. Even if someone in authority points out a behavior of yours that they do not like, you have the right to defend yourself and to be treated fairly. Here are some guidelines for accepting criticism:

1. Listen. Don't try to interrupt or defend yourself until you know exactly what the problem is. Breathing deeply will help you stay calm and pay attention.
2. Repeat the criticism in your own words so you are sure you have the facts right. This helps you both understand exactly what's involved, and it also gives you a moment to calm down.
3. Ask for a specific example of what is being criticized.
4. Decide for yourself whether the criticism is fair. Is it factual? Is it something you can or want to correct?
5. If the criticism is fair, don't give excuses. Instead, think of ways you can do things differently or ask the person, "What would you like me to do to correct this problem?"
6. If the criticism is unfair, start with "I" statements; for example, "I

feel misunderstood," or "I feel unable to meet your expectations." Avoid using "you" statements that accuse or insult: "You don't understand the situation" or "You're being unfair about this" or "You really don't know what you're talking about."

7. The encounter may make you angry and tempt you to wage a counterattack. That would be unfortunate. If you feel out of control, you could ask the person to postpone the discussion until a time when you feel calmer and can think more clearly and objectively.

Criticism very often catches us off guard. So, once you realize you are being criticized, try to stay calm, breathe deeply, and pay close attention to what is being said. Criticism is not always unfair, and often we can use it to improve ourselves and our work.

On the other hand, criticism is sometimes unfounded. You have to be able to distinguish between realistic and unfounded criticism and stand up for yourself when you feel you have been criticized unjustly. You have the right to defend yourself and to act only on criticism that you believe is on target.

ACCEPTING COMPLIMENTS

A lot of people feel as uneasy receiving positive, warm expressions, such as compliments, as they do receiving criticism. Many people brush compliments off, embarrassed, with an offhanded remark like "Oh, this old sweater—I just dragged it out of the closet this morning." You may think you are being modest when you respond this way, but you are actually putting the other person down by suggesting that he or she was either not serious or said something trivial.

Compliments are often handled on two levels, internal and external. The external level is the simpler of the two. A simple "Thank-you" or a more generous response such as "I'm so happy you noticed!" is often enough. Straightforward, gracious acceptance of a compliment shows the other person that you heard their opinion and that you value it. However, if you really do have difficulty accepting a compliment, say so. For example: "Compliments make me feel uncomfortable, but I do appreciate that you said that." The key here is to be yourself, to express your honest feelings.

The second level of accepting compliments is internal. This can often be difficult, especially when a compliment touches on matters that are deeply personal. The tendency is to block the compliment so that it is not internalized. If you feel uncomfortable a simple thank-you will suffice, but later, try to understand what it is that blocks you from accepting other people's genuine positive reactions to you and your behavior.

HANDLING CONFLICT SITUATIONS

Many people approach conflict situations with some faulty assumptions. See whether yours are among these:

1. In any conflict, one party is right and one party is wrong— there's no in between.
2. You must win in every situation.
3. Every conflict must be fully resolved.
4. Your solution is the only worthwhile one.
5. Only the person who is right may get what he or she wants.
6. With compromise, someone always winds up feeling the loser.
7. If you can't succeed in resolving a conflict, you must be inadequate.

All of these statements are flawed. As in all assertive interactions, the key here is to do your best to resolve the conflict and still respect your own and the other person's feelings. All conflicts do not have to be resolved fully or in a single discussion. Some conflicts can be resolved through compromise that leaves both parties feeling that they have won, or at least arrived at a resolution both can live with.

ARE YOU READY FOR ASSERTIVENESS?

You can reverse nonassertive or aggressive tendencies by starting small, with people with whom you already feel comfortable. For example, you may have strong feelings about national politics, but you keep them to yourself because others may not agree with you or because you do not know whether your opinions are valid. If an opportunity arises while you are among friends, perhaps with co-workers at lunch, offer an opinion and watch the reaction of the others. With practice, you will feel more at ease expressing yourself.

Here are some common questions and concerns that many people have about the benefits and consequences of adopting an assertive style:

Question: I'm afraid that if I assert myself with my supervisor, he or she will get angry and I'll get fired. Is this a realistic concern?
Answer: Nobody can predict another person's reaction, but even if your supervisor does get angry, with calm assertiveness you can continue the discussion in a constructive way. Imagine how much worse the situation would be if you became aggressive, not assertive. In that case, your actions might lead to disciplinary action or termination. In any event, like anyone else, your supervisor is responsible for his or her own responses, and if he or she becomes unreasonably angry, you must remind yourself that this is not your fault.

Question: If I assert myself with my co-workers, will they still like me?
Answer: People make their own choices about whom they like or dislike. Being liked may be a worthwhile personal goal, but it should not be pursued at the expense of your self-respect. When you are assertive, you attract people with self-respect and respect for others— probably the kind of people you want as friends. Also, you will learn to like yourself

better so that being liked by everyone becomes less important.

Question: Will my customers be offended if I speak up to them?
Answer: Most people appreciate directness. Of course, that doesn't mean that you can be rude or insensitive; that would be aggressive, not assertive behavior. But honesty and directness tempered with concern and consideration are not likely to be so harsh that most customers will become angry. In fact, they may very well appreciate your honesty.

Question: Should I always strive to meet every need of others?
Answer: Nobody can be all things to all people. All that is asked of you is that you do the best you can. To allow anyone to treat you disrespectfully is not constructive. For instance, if a physician yelled at you because he wants to pressure you to stop whatever you are doing so you can help him, instead of taking it passively, you could say, "When you calm down, I know I can help you."

Question: Suppose I need to place limits on a patient's behavior, and the patient becomes angry as a result. Shouldn't I take that to mean that the patient's anger is my fault?
Answer: No. Every person—every patient, every co-worker, every doctor or supervisor you work with—is responsible for his or her own feelings and reactions. If your patient is angry because of your actions and you know that your actions are in everyone's best interest, then you have a right to stand your ground. You can persist in helping the patient to understand the need for the limits and show empathy for his or her feelings even if you disagree. For example, "I can imagine your frustration when you received another bland meal, but I want you to recuperate and this diet is going to help."

Question: Will assertiveness make me appear cold and uncaring?
Answer: Some people who want you to be passive and accommodating at all costs to yourself may indeed accuse you of being cold and uncaring. You can't let their accusations throw you off balance. Remind yourself that you were respectful when you were assertive and that they're merely trying to push you to reverse your decisions. Assertiveness only means that you are taking better care of yourself. To some people that may mean that they are no longer able to manipulate and take advantage of you. Others will be delighted to see you being assertive, and they may actually see you as more caring and more accessible. Once again, people

are responsible for their own reactions. Assertiveness used well gives you the confidence and courage you need to withstand whatever negative reactions you may encounter. You'll know that you took the high road in your behavior.

Question: If I am going to assert myself and voice my thoughts and opinions, people might challenge me. What if I don't have the facts to back up everything I've said?

Answer: Being assertive doesn't mean that you have all the answers all the time. Opinions, for example, don't always have to be backed up with facts—they're just an expression of how you feel about something. Being assertive doesn't mean being right all the time, either. Some people find it difficult to say "I don't know." But to say it directly and honestly is assertive and a sign of strength. As much as anyone else, you are entitled not to have all the answers all the time.

It's time to test your personal beliefs about your own effectiveness in dealing with others. Use the next exercise to see how assertive and how confident you have become.

ASSERTIVENESS SUCCESS VISUALIZATION
Instructions: Simply follow the steps.
This exercise is designed to help you get past your fear of acting assertively. The objective is to imagine how you could react to a particular situation in an assertive way. You may role-play the situation with a friend or co-worker, but you should also practice by yourself when you are relaxed and not distracted.
1. Think of a situation in which you want to become more assertive. Concentrate on the total situation and think of all the most important details—who you are with, what you will say, and what the other person will say and do. Your first visualization of this situation should reflect what you would typically do.
2. Next, imagine yourself speaking assertively in the same situation. Think about what you would say and how you would look and act, and feel yourself acting confident and assertive.

3. Concentrate deeply on the situation, and review every assertive detail. Think about eye contact, your posture, the tone and volume of your voice, your gestures, and about your total appearance to the other person. Pinpoint every aspect of yourself as you are feeling assertive.

4. Now imagine the responses of the other person, what he or she says and does. Are you creating a realistic picture? Be aware of your own feelings as this imaginary other person reacts to your assertiveness.

5. Imagine another outcome to this encounter—the other person responds to your assertive behavior in a neutral or negative way. What would the person be doing or saying? Would such a neutral or negative response be likely? How do you feel inside as a result of this other person's neutral or negative response? Are you hurt? Angry? Does it really matter to your self-esteem that this person does not approve of your assertive behavior?

6. Regardless of the other person's reactions, you want to reward yourself for being assertive and for standing up for what you believe. How would you reward yourself? How would that make you feel?

7. You've been assertive—now feel good about it! Enjoy it. Tell yourself how good it feels to be assertive.

8. Resolve to translate your assertive fantasies into real-life situations.

ASSERTIVENESS/EFFECTIVENESS SCALE

Instructions: Read each of the statements and circle the number from five to one that best describes you. A one means that the statement definitely describes you and a 5 means that it never describes you.

		DEFINITELY "ME"			NOT AT ALL "ME	
1.	When I'm working with my customers, I put my own	1	2	3	4	5

		1	2	3	4	5
	feelings aside and concentrate only on what they want.					
2.	I hate it when people become angry with me, so I keep my feelings to myself.	1	2	3	4	5
3.	I care about getting the job done, but it's more important that people like me.	1	2	3	4	5
4.	I know I'd be able to succeed if the people around me weren't so stupid and incompetent.	1	2	3	4	5

5.	I deserve better	1	2	3	4	5
6.	In my personal life, other people come first. Their needs are more important than my own	1	2	3	4	5
7.	I should do	1	2	3	4	5
8.	I should do exactly what my customers want, even if my supervisor doesn't want me to do it	1	2	3	4	5
9.	I don't believe in talking about my successes and achievements because I don't want people	1	2	3	4	5

		1	2	3	4	5
	to think I'm conceited					
10.	I get really irritated when people don't agree with my opinions	1	2	3	4	5
11.	I keep my opinions to myself because I don't want other people to think I'm odd or stupid or that I disagree with them.	1	2	3	4	5
12.	I think the way to deal with people who disagree with me is to belittle and make fun of them.	1	2	3	4	5
13.	Nobody	1	2	3	4	5

	has any right to criticize me.					
14.	When someone	1	2	3	4	5
15.	I tend to be sarcastic.	1	2	3	4	5
	TOTAL					

Your Score: If you scored high on this test, you need to change some of your beliefs in order to become more assertive. If you gave high scores to statements 4, 5, 10, 12 and 15, you are likely to show a tendency toward aggressive behavior. The remaining statements indicate that you have strong nonassertive tendencies. Study your current tendencies carefully and pinpoint ways you can change them.

Summary

You are unique. There is no other person who looks like you or has your mix of intellect, talents, skills and experiences. No one has exactly the same set of opinions, cares and needs as you do. All these qualities are what make you a unique and special individual. However, nobody can know what you think or what you care about until you express yourself.

Because you are unique and because your thinking is unique, you have a lot to offer everyone around you. You can help people see things in a different way. You can help them understand you and themselves better and sometimes even make important changes by telling them how you feel about them—and how you feel about your own life. You can influence others, including your co-workers and patients, but only if you assert yourself through your words, your feelings, your opinions, and your actions.

Being assertive does not mean that you must be selfish. Getting what you want does not mean getting it at the expense of other people or taking something away from someone else. Assertiveness means being true to yourself, letting people around you know who you are, and giving them the opportunity to like you, to work with you, and to respect you—for what you have to offer, for your uniqueness, and for your true value. Assertiveness is simply another way of taking control of your life. Becoming assertive will take practice, but when you are comfortable asserting yourself and taking more control you may find that you are happier about your work as well as about other areas of your life.

FURTHER READING ON ASSERTIVENESS

- Buckley, CD., and Walker, D., *Harmony: Professional Renewal for Nurses*. Chicago: American Hospital Publishing, 1989.
- Clark, C. C, *Assertive Skills for Nurses*. Wakefield, Mass.: Contemporary Publishing, 1978.
- Jakubowski, P., and Lange, A. J., *The Assertive Option: Your Rights and Responsibilities*. Champaign, 111.: Research Press Company, 1978.
- Lloyd,S. R., *Developing Positive Assertiveness: Practical Techniques for Personal Success*. Los Altos, Calif.: Crisp Publications, 1988.

Best-Selling Books by Wendy Leebov, Ed.D.

http://www.quality-patient-experience.com/wendy-leebov-books.html

Physician Entrepreneurs: The Quality Patient Experience -- Improve outcomes, boost quality scores, and increase revenue *(Book and CD-2008)* Built around the key areas in the CAHPS survey, this book and tool-packed CD offers quick and easy techniques that physicians and practice staff can use to enhance the patient experience—without sacrificing productivity.

Wendy Leebov's Essentials for Great Patient Experiences: No Nonsense Solutions with Gratifying Results *(2008)* Specific tools that enhance the patient experience and address the difficulties staff have in delivering the exemplary care they would like to provide. High-impact strategies for moving your service excellence and patient satisfaction to a new level, resulting in higher scores on HCAHPS and CG-CAHPS.

Wendy Leebov's Essentials for Great Personal Leadership: No Nonsense Solutions with Gratifying Results *(2008)* Valuable problem-solving and leadership development for health care executives, mid-level administrators, department heads, clinical leaders, and anyone who brings a passion to their work. Each chapter captures the essence of emotionally intelligent leadership and focuses on effective solutions.

Service Quality Improvement: The Customer Satisfaction Strategy for Health Care *(Leebov and Scott)* A goldmine of approaches for your service excellence initiative, that helps you build a service-oriented culture and focusing all employees on service excellence and continuous service improvement.

The Indispensable Health Care Manager: Success Strategies for a Changing Environment *(Leebov and Scott - 2003 Health Care Book of the Year)* Identifies ten role shifts needed by managers who want to add significant value to their organizations and enhance their employability. Self-assessments, case situations and concrete tools that build key leadership competencies.

Also by Wendy Leebov—practical guides that help frontline employees provide the exceptional patient and family experience

- Assertiveness Skills for Professionals in Health Care

- Customer Service for Professionals in Health Care

- Telephone Skills for Professionals in Health Care

- Resolving Complaints for Professionals in Health Care

- Working Together for Professionals in Health Care

Enrich Your Tools and Confidently Guide Your Team to the Next Level

http://www.quality-patient-experience.com/wendy-leebov-books.html

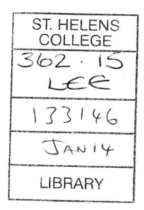
CPSIA information can be obtained at www.ICGtesting.com
Printed in the USA
LVOW06s1613171013

357413LV00015B/1099/P

9 781479 336067